Thoughts
Unwritten

Tofiyinfun Salawu

About the Author

Tofiyinfun Salawu, known as Tofi, writes with honesty and emotion. Thoughts Unwritten is a raw reflection of the moments and feelings she's lived through those times that don't come with easy answers or perfect endings. Her words explore what it means to grow, to struggle, and to keep going even when everything feels heavy.

She lives in Prosper, Texas, and spends her time running, capturing life through photographs, and being surrounded by family, the kind of presence that brings both peace and grounding. Though her life is comfortable, there's rarely a moment when her mind isn't thinking, wondering, or reflecting. Her writing speaks to anyone who's ever felt stuck in their own thoughts or unsure of what's next.

Thoughts Unwritten may be the first, but it won't be the last.

The Teaser

Unwritten Thoughts was written to express the emotions I couldn't vocalize. Hence, it acts as a voice for anyone who might be struggling with similar challenges. I hope whoever is reading this book realizes that it's okay to not be okay, to feel like you are under a boulder, but it's never okay to hide those thoughts and emotions away from the world. Every thought that you carry in your mind is amazing and unique in its own way, as it represents you and your individuality.

To the people who believed in this book when I didn't: my dad, my family, and my close friend, Ogechi Nwankwo.

Table of Contents

Chapter 1:
Perfection Within My Body

The concept of perfection is not merely a word or a feeling. It is not a tone or a sound. Neither is it something material that can be bought, borrowed, or handed to you. We've seen perfection throughout history, seen how hard it is to maintain, and yet people still chase after it as if it's something tangible. Contrary to how people take it, perfection is the sense of lightness you experience when you've reached a lofty goal that you never thought you could achieve. It's that small moment of peace when everything feels like it's in the right place. When some people hear the word perfection, they immediately think of doubt and fear. They think of the pressure to be something they're not, the weight of expectations pressing down on them until they can't breathe. But that's not the right way to think about it. Perfection isn't about comparison. It isn't about fear. It isn't about being better than someone else. Perfection is simply finding and achieving the path you take toward a better life. It's about growth, about pushing yourself in a way that feels right for you. That is how you should perceive the essence of perfection. However, in today's reality, perfection is not seen as something personal or meaningful. It's no more about how you feel on the inside; it's more about how you look on the outside. It's about appearance, about how well you fit into a standard that someone else created. Where you come from, how you speak, how you carry yourself, these things are judged before anyone cares to understand the person behind them. Being slim, wearing makeup, and dressing a certain way have become the norms, the rules that determine whether someone is seen as worthy of admiration. But why does it have to be that way? Why can't perfection be about what you are or what you aspire to be? Why can't it be about you feeling comfortable in your own skin, no matter what that looks like? It's important to love yourself, regardless of anything. Regardless of what the world says, regardless of what people think, regardless of how many times you've been told you need to change. The true definition of perfection is loving yourself and being true to who you are. Something that only you can see.

Only you.

Chapter 2:
The Truth

How do I explain the truth when no one wants to hear it? People say the truth has two sides, but it doesn't. It's one thing, unchanging, no matter how much we try to twist it. The truth can't be shaped and tailored according to what feels right. Even if it doesn't feel right to you, even if it makes you uncomfortable, the truth stays the same. Without the cold, hard facts, it never fully comes to light. It stays hidden, waiting for its moment. Maybe that's why it's so hard for us to accept, why we look for other versions to believe, because the real truth? That's the one that asks the most of us. It's bound to make us uncomfortable, but in the end, it always gives us light.

Chapter 3:
A Call to Hold On

Don't be the reason a beautiful soul takes their own life. Words have weight. Actions have consequences. You never know what someone is silently battling, what thoughts linger in their mind when the world grows quiet. In honor of Suicide Prevention Month, I want to remind you of something that often gets overlooked: It's okay to not be okay, but it's not okay to let that pain convince you that your life isn't worth living. I understand deeply what it feels like not to want to be alive on this earth anymore. I've wrestled with this overwhelming battle within myself for years, trapped in a cycle of thoughts that felt too heavy to carry. There were moments I believed the darkness would swallow me whole, moments where the idea of relief seemed impossible. I know what it's like to wake up and feel nothing, to go to sleep wishing you wouldn't wake up at all. But I also know that those feelings, as unbearable as they seem, do not define the rest of your life. I've lost friends to the darkness of suicidal thoughts, and the ache of wishing I could go back to give them one last hug, one last call, one last reason to hold on, never leaves me. The regret of wondering if I could have said something different, if I could have reminded them one more time that they mattered, weighs on my heart. The pain of losing someone that way never goes away; it lingers in the silence, in the moments where you find yourself staring at old photos, rereading old messages, wondering how things could have turned out differently, only if you could have said or done something to save them. Suicide doesn't just take one life; it shatters the lives of everyone left behind. The pain can be suffocating, and the survival may look like a long-lost dream, but I promise you this: there is always a chance for a brighter side, even if it feels far away. There is always a possibility for change, for healing, for something beyond the pain you feel right now. Please, reach out even if it's just a whisper. Even if it's just a text. Even if it's just a moment of honesty with yourself. You're never truly alone, no matter how isolated you might feel. The road ahead is long, and it's worth every step, even the hardest ones. You don't have to have it all figured out right now. You don't have to pretend you're okay when you're not. But you do have to hold on. Because there are still moments waiting for your laughter, you haven't experienced, places you haven't seen, love you haven't felt, and a future that is still yours to create and cherish.

Chapter 4:
Eyes that Shine

How can I describe the feeling I get when I see you, how my heart lifts just enough to remind me that something good is about to start? More than overwhelming, it's bright, like sunlight filtering through the trees: soft, warm, and easy. I'm happy when I see you, and this happiness feels fresh, untangled, and full of quiet joy. I feel like a field of flowers, not yet in full bloom but steadily growing toward something beautiful. It's a feeling I don't want to question. What can I call it? Excitement? It's not love, but it's something real and full of potential. Every time I see you, I let myself meet your eyes, without hesitation. It doesn't bring pain or confusion, just this light that makes me want to see where it leads. When our eyes meet, it feels like there's something worth exploring, and I don't need to hold back. It's not perfect, but it's more than enough for now...

Chapter 5:
We Accept the Love We Think We Deserve

In the shadows of our quiet thoughts, we settle for a love that mirrors our own image, a love shaped by the echo of our own self-worth, however fragile. We accept love in fragments, in quiet glances and half-meant words, because we think that's all we're worth. It's a delicate bargain, comforted by a familiar pain, where we hesitate to reach for more, fearing the risk of disappointment. But in reality, love isn't a measure of who we are now but who we might become if only we allowed ourselves to believe we're worthy of something greater, something wholesome. It's a choice to break the pattern, to step beyond what we think we deserve, and to open ourselves to the full bloom of love that waits, undemanding, just beyond our own doubts.

Chapter 6:
Dreams Deferred

Dreams don't always fade; they just wait. From childhood to the teenage years, they're vivid and electric, full of promise, yet they feel so distant and empty, like a road with no trail. I can see it, but I cannot take it. At the current moment, the top and most important goal is to follow school and focus on grades. It's about staying on track and planning for some distant future. The thing that doesn't occur to us is that we can feel those dreams inside us, a little spark that never leaves. We cannot ignore them. Someday, they'll become more than just thoughts in our heads and transform into true aspirations. Eventually, someday, they'll become our reality.

Chapter 7:
The Room I'm Not In

The pictures flood my screen, each one a piece of a world I wasn't invited into. Smiling faces, inside jokes, and fleeting moments captured in frames where my name doesn't belong. It isn't jealousy, just this reminder of all the rooms I'm in. It's not about this one event, though. My absence will echo louder than anything I've ever said, and the world will move on without me. But then, I wonder how many times I've missed the room I'm already standing in, chasing one that wasn't meant for me? How many moments have slipped through my fingers because I was staring at everyone else's? Maybe the fear of missing out isn't really fear at all, just a distraction. And maybe, just maybe, where I am right now is enough.

Chapter 8:
The Ties That Bind

Family is a complicated mix of love, tension, and roles we never asked for but somehow fit into. It's the tightrope we walk on, balancing expectations, emotions, and unspoken truths, knowing which buttons not to press and which silences speak the loudest. But even through the mess, the arguments, the fragile moments, and the unfairness, there's love in the smallest gestures: saving the last piece of cake, a quiet apology, or a shared laugh. It doesn't always make sense, but it's the one thing you always come back to.

Chapter 9:
The Aspect of Being Weird

Being weird isn't something you choose; it's just something you have been since the day you were created. It's the way your thoughts never quite match the crowd, how you laugh too loud at the wrong moments, or how your interests never align with everyone else's. At first, being weird feels like a spotlight, shining on every awkward quirk, every mismatched outfit, every joke that lands with the force of a brick. You feel like the main character in a sitcom where the laugh track malfunctions at the worst moments. But after a while, you realize it's not a spotlight, it's just your shadow. And maybe it's time to stop running from it. After all, you can't outrun yourself–unless you're being chased by a wasp, in which case, I fully support sprinting like your life depends on it. Weird isn't bad. It's the pieces of you that can't be replaced, the parts that don't fit the mold because they were never meant to. However, they're the ones that make your puzzle look complete. Think about it, every "normal" person in history is probably forgotten, but the weird ones? The ones who thought outside the box, colored outside the lines, danced when there was no music? Those are the people who left a mark. And let's be real, if being weird was such a bad thing, why do people spend billions of dollars every year trying to be "unique"? You're out here being naturally weird for free. That's a talent. Sure, it might be lonely at times.

Sometimes you'll crack a joke that only you find funny, and sometimes you'll reference a book or movie and be met with the blankest of stares. But there's also a certain freedom in not fitting in everywhere. No one expects you to follow trends when they already assume you're five steps ahead... or ten steps to the side, doing your own thing entirely.

Chapter 10:
Death Is a Long Story

No one ever thinks about the weight of silence after loss, how it fills the spaces where laughter and love once lived. The experience of grief is a long story that never truly ends, a reminder of everything you've lost and the life you once lived. I cannot explain the feeling or pain of seeing the person you cared about most in this world die right in front of you, unable to do anything but cry through the screen. Hearing their tears and screams is a nightmare that replays endlessly, a wound that never fully heals. It's the kind of sound that stays with you forever not in a memory you cherish, but in a trauma that haunts. You never forget that sound of shrieks and grief. The heartbreak in their voice. The fear. The pain. The silence that followed. You never forget the way your own voice cracked as you begged them to hold on, knowing deep down there was nothing left to hold onto. Death is a long story, full of chapters we don't choose to write, and in order to live through its path, we must walk it step by step, day by day, carrying the echoes of what was and the hope of what might still be. But nobody talks about how heavily draining the process can get. Nobody talks about how exhausting it is to wake up every day and pretend like you're okay. Pretend like the world didn't just rip the one person you loved out of your hands. Pretend like you're supposed to keep moving forward when everything in you is stuck in that moment, stuck staring at a screen, stuck hearing their last words, stuck in the silence that followed after the soul left their body. Nobody talks about how grief changes you; how it makes you bitter; how it makes you angry; how it makes you tired in a way that even sleep can't fix it. How it makes you distant, numb, hollow. How it makes everything feel pointless. Death is a long story. And I'm still in the middle of it. Still stuck on the same fucking page. Still staring at the same scene that I've read a million times, hoping it'll change, knowing it never will. And maybe it never gets easier. Maybe it's not supposed to. Maybe some losses are just too big. Maybe some people aren't meant to be gotten over.

Maybe grief just becomes a part of you. Not something you heal from. Not something you fix. Just something you carry. Quietly. Always.

Chapter 11:
Chasing the Pace

There's this constant drive inside me to be better, to push past the limits I've set for myself and reach something more. Every race and every practice feels like a test, and the clock ticks faster than I can breathe, reminding me that time is always slipping away. I feel behind, like I'm always just a few steps away from catching up, and I wonder if I'll ever close that distance. When I run, everything else disappears. The world outside the track fades away with the passing wind. Life problems, school stress, the weight of expectations, all of it is drowned out by the rhythm of my feet pounding against the ground. But still, I know that the only way to truly escape is to be faster. To outpace my doubts, my insecurities, and my limitations. Life feels like a similar race sometimes, and the faster I get, the more I feel like I can catch up to it. But no matter how fast I run, I'm always trying to stay ahead of what's chasing me, of all the things I can't control. I need to run, not just for the release, but because the faster I get, the further I can leave the chaos behind.

Chapter 12:
A Little Faith

There are times when the world feels too overwhelming, and it's hard to know where to turn. In those moments, the thought of God is like a quiet whisper that reminds you you're not alone. I remember when I got baptized, it never really hit me what it meant until I realized that sometimes, all you need is just a little faith without it making sense to you. It wasn't about the ceremony or the outward act; it was about trusting in an entity way bigger than myself, something that could carry me through the rough patches. God isn't always the answer you expect, but the peace that comes from believing, even in uncertainty. It is like letting go of the breath you didn't know you were holding. In the darkest moments, it's that faith, that quiet assurance, that keeps you going, even when everything else seems uncertain.

Chapter 13:
The Power of Laughter

Laughter is a strange thing. It can feel like a momentary escape, even when everything else is closing in on you. Sometimes, it's a sudden burst, unexpected, like a flicker of light in a dark room. It's fleeting, though, and it quickly fades, again leaving behind the weight of whatever was pressing down before. But even in those short, sweet moments, there's something beautiful about it. Laughter connects people in a way nothing else can, reminding everyone that even in the hardest times, there's a bit of light left to hold onto. It doesn't make the pain disappear, but it makes it bearable for a while, and that's enough. The sadness returns, as it always does, but laughter, no matter how brief, reminds the heart that joy is still possible, even when the weight of the world feels too much to carry.

Chapter 14:
The Memory of a Smile

There are days when all you can remember is someone's smile. It's not the grand moments that stay with you, but the small things, the way their eyes lit up when they saw you, the warmth in their laugh. That smile stays with you even after they're gone, a reminder of something that once was. You catch yourself replaying it in your mind, hoping that one day, you'll get to see it again. And though you know time moves on, that smile keeps you tethered to a time and place that can never return. You learn that some memories become more precious when they're all you have left.

Chapter 15:
Food, Glorious Food!

Food isn't just something we eat; it's a full-on adventure. Take breakfast; those first bites of pancakes drenched in syrup? Suddenly, you're on a beach in Hawaii, even if you're sitting in your kitchen, wearing yesterday's clothes with a coffee stain on your shirt. Then there's lunch, that magical moment when you're too tired to care about life, but a sandwich or burrito transforms into a five-star meal. You bite into it, and suddenly you're an explorer in a savory jungle, fighting off wild hunger with the power of a taco. But dinner, oh, dinner is the grand finale. You plan it like you're throwing a banquet, even if it's just spaghetti. But when that sauce hits the noodles? You feel like you're dining in Italy with a chef who won't stop telling you how amazing you are, even though all you did was boil pasta and hoped for the best. And dessert? That's where things get out of hand. A slice of chocolate cake? Boom! Food isn't just food, it's an all-expense-paid trip to somewhere wonderful, even if that somewhere is just your couch. It's not just about the taste; it's a wholesome experience. A bite of bliss that makes everything feel right, even if only for a few minutes… before you start thinking about what to have for breakfast tomorrow.

Chapter 16:
Friendship

There are friends who come into your life like a bright light, and even when they're gone, the warmth they left never fades. The laughter shared, the late-night talks, the moments of silence where words weren't needed, those are the memories that stick with you. Some friendships stay, and some slip away with time, but the impact they leave is everlasting. It's not the time spent together that matters, but the way they changed you, made you feel seen, and showed up when you needed it most. No matter how much distance grows between you, true friendship is never really gone. It lingers, tucked away in quiet corners of your heart, reminding you that love, even in its quietest form, never truly leaves. And maybe I only know how real that feels because, truthfully, I've never really had friends. Not in the way people talk about. Not in the way people post about. Not in the way people casually mention their group chats or their weekend plans or the friends they call just to talk about nothing. For me, friendship has always been Sosena. My source of joy. My ride or die. My safe space. My person. She's been that light in my life, the only one who ever stayed long enough for me to call her home. But if I'm being honest… me and her don't really talk as much as we used to. Life got busy. Things changed. The calls got fewer, and the texts less often. But even with all that distance, even with all that space between us now, she's still that person for me. She always will be. Nothing is going to change that. But outside of her? It's always just been me. I know what it's like to be lonely. To scroll through your phone and realize there's no one to text. No one to call. No one to make plans with. No random "let's hang out" texts. No late-night calls just because. Just... silence. I know what it feels like to sit in your room and wonder what's so wrong with you that friendships never stick. To wonder why everyone else seems to have people. People to laugh with, people to cry with, people to just exist with, and I don't. Even now, to this day, I still feel lonely. I still don't have friends like that. I still don't have a group chat waiting for me. I still don't have anyone to call when life gets too heavy. It hurts. It's a different kind of hurt. The kind you learn to live with because you have no choice. And maybe friendship really is just a concept for me. A beautiful idea that I only know from the outside looking in. Something I've felt pieces of through Sosena, but never fully had in the way I've always wanted. But even so... those moments, those memories, those rare pieces of love, they stay with me. And maybe that's enough. Perhaps, it has to be.

Chapter 17:
I Cannot Communicate but I Try

There are moments when communication feels like talking in a foreign language, one you can't quite grasp, no matter how hard you try. The words are there, bouncing around in your head, but they never quite make sense. They get stuck in the space between your thoughts and your mouth, and no matter how much you push, they won't come. It's like trying to reach someone through a glass wall, your words are on the other side, but the distance makes them fall short. You try, you really do, to connect, to make sense of what's inside, but there's a disconnect, a crack that can't be fixed with a little more effort. Sometimes, the silence speaks louder than the words you can't find. "I'm sorry if it feels like I'm not trying, but I am, and deep down, I hope you know I am." You wish you could explain, wish you could make them understand, but in the end, you are just stuck in a cycle of trying again and again, even when it feels like it's never enough. Because maybe that's all you can do, keep reaching, even when it feels like you're not getting anywhere.

Chapter 18
The Comfort of Sleep

Sleep is the escape we all need but rarely appreciate until we've gone without it. It's the place where the mind can finally rest, where the world fades, and the weight of the day slips away. But sleep isn't just about rest; it's where the thoughts that kept you up at night go to find their peace. Sometimes, sleep feels like the only place where things make sense, even if just for a few hours. In the quiet of the night, the dreams take over, and for a brief moment, everything is still. Yet, it's in those moments of rest that we're reminded how fragile we are, how desperately we need to stop, to breathe, and let go of everything just for a while. And when the morning comes, we wake up, not always feeling completely whole, but with enough strength to try again.

Chapter 19
When Silence Speaks

Sometimes, you just gotta let the silence do the talking, even when you have a million things to say. There are moments when words fail you, when you're standing there with so much inside, but nothing seems to fit. It's like the weight of your thoughts is too much for your mouth to carry. And in those moments, silence can be the loudest thing in the room. It speaks volumes, not in words, but in the spaces between them. It's the way you sit next to someone, letting the quiet fill the space instead of trying to force a conversation. It's the kind of silence that says, "I understand," even when you don't. Because sometimes, silence is the only thing that makes sense, and in its quiet, it can carry the truth you can't find the words for.

Chapter 20:
Why Would I Write This Book?

There are days when the thought of putting all these emotions, these untold stories, into words seems impossible. Like the weight of it all would crush the paper if I tried to capture it in words. Why would anyone care about the thoughts, the struggles, the moments that feel too personal, too raw to expose to the world? The fear of being misunderstood, the fear of judgment, the fear that the words won't land the way they're supposed to, it's overwhelming.

But then, in the quiet, when the weight of everything becomes a little too much to carry alone, it becomes clear. This book isn't just for me. It never was. It's for anyone who's ever felt misunderstood. Anyone who's ever felt lost in their own thoughts, drowning in feelings they can't put into words. It's for the people who stay silent because their voice feels too small, too weak, too insignificant. It's for the ones who keep their pain locked away, because no one ever told them it was okay to speak it out loud. Writing this book is a way to say, "I get it." It's a way to reach out to the people who feel invisible, who feel like no one sees them for who they really are. It's a way to give voice to the silent struggles, the hidden battles that no one else talks about. These are the words that nobody else could find, the thoughts no one else could piece together, the feelings that get lost in the noise of the world. Sometimes it feels like we're all just stumbling through life, trying to make sense of a world that's so chaotic, so overwhelming. We're all carrying our own invisible weight, and sometimes, it's easy to believe we're the only ones. The loneliness in that thought is suffocating. But writing this and sharing these sentiments is a way of telling others, "You're not alone." Maybe this book won't change the world. Maybe it won't be some groundbreaking revelation that shifts the way people think. But if it helps just one person feel seen, heard, or understood, if it gives someone the courage to speak their truth, to finally say what they've been holding in, then maybe, just maybe, it has achieved its purpose. Because sometimes, all we need is to know that someone else understands. That someone else has been there. That someone else has felt the weight of it all and survived. And if this book can give that to even one person, then every word will have been worth it.

Chapter 21:
Goodbye

And just like that, it's time to close this chapter. Not because the story is over, but because it's time to let go, to move forward, and to trust that the next step is waiting. These pages were never meant to have all the answers, but to share the journey, the struggles, the growth. To remind us that we're not alone, even when it feels like we are. So, here's the goodbye, not as an ending, but as a pause. A pause to reflect, to carry what's been shared here into the next part of the journey. The words have been said, the thoughts have been put out there, and now it's time to see where they lead. Thank you for reading, for sharing this space. You were never just a reader, you were a part of this, too. And though this book ends, the story doesn't. The journey continues, as do we. So, goodbye for now. But not forever!

Where the Unspoken Finds a Home

These pages are yours. Say what you feel, what you've been holding in, or what you've never had the space to express.

_____

_____

_____

_____

_____

_____

_____

_____

_____

_____

_____

_____

_____

_____

_____

_____

_____

www.ingramcontent.com/pod-product-compliance
Lightning Source LLC
Chambersburg PA
CBHW051250120626
46547CB00014B/1878